ideals® EASTER

Along comes April!
Her springtime air
calls us to slow and linger there.
For the earth once more has come to life
to echo His loving sacrifice.
—SUSAN SUNDWALL

ideals
NASHVILLE, TENNESSEE

I Love a Little Growing Thing

Edna Jaques

I love a little growing thing
that sticks his nose up in the spring
above the cold and frozen ground
when there is nothing
    much around.

A tiny bush brave as a knight
whose little leaves are rolled up tight,
who dares to tell them to unfold
in spite of icy winds and cold.

A crocus dressed in fuzzy fur
who felt the life within it stir,
and, lo, a flower poked its head
above a frozen flower bed.

A bush that wintered by the well
with such a fairytale to tell,
of dreams within its shiny bark,
of voices whispering in the dark.

For life can hold such shining hours,
new budded trees and scarlet flowers,
the blessed faith in life that springs
from the deep heart of
    growing things.

It's Easter

Thomas Curtis Clark

When winter winds have spent
    their force
and March snows melt away,
when morning dawns with
    sunny cheer
and friends make glad the day,
when faith returns to
    grieving hearts
and hope is born again,
when happy bluebirds stir
    their nest
and life becomes a thrilling quest—
it's Easter.

When greening meadows
    show a path
for vagrant feet to roam,
when in the garden jonquils peep
and lilies burst the loam,
when there come thoughts of
    One who rose
from darkness of the tomb,
when life is sweet and hope
    is strong
and every heart is filled
    with song—
it's Easter.

EASTER EGG HUNT *I by Bob Pettes. Image ©*
Bob Pettes/Porterfield's Fine Art Licensing

Easter Morning, County Line Road

Deborah A. Bennett

There are places high on the hills that are still white with ice and snow this Easter morning. On this, our first day without hat or boots, I carry out sunflower seeds for the birds, who sit everywhere in the trees as if they have been waiting to be fed. Four or five jostle one another on the limbs of an ash tree. Though I know they won't come near the seeds until I am gone, I watch the way the wind ruffles their feathers for a while and I swallow a wish to fly up and sit next to them.

A woodpecker's drumming from the branch of an oak tree mixes with flute-like notes to create a sound happier than on any other Easter dawn I can remember. I follow the footpath around our backyard pond, stepping on leaves that fell here in the fall. The water's edge is a brown sludge. The neighbor's golden retriever has discovered something interesting rustling in a patch of lemongrass. Once on the shore, he satisfies the urge to roll around in what must be delicious mud.

There will be flowers blooming here soon, like little girls in Easter dresses, and blackberries on the bank by June or July. The birds will soon

Early spring in Cades Cove area of Great Smoky Mountains National Park, Tennessee. Photograph © Mary Liz Austin/Donnelly-Austin Photography

devour cherries from the trees like candy, as well as strawberries from the vines. With green and noble manes full of dust and dew, the yucca plants my mother planted over thirty years ago are evergreen. The plant whose name I do not know is sprouting leaves like little tied-together canoes.

The wind speaks through the trees with the tender tones of a mother waking a child from a troublesome sleep. The sun rises and guides a wide wheel of light over a patch of newborn grass, and the whole world turns greener and greener before my eyes. A flock of blackbirds feasts on the sprinkle of sunflower seed I left back on the hill, under the trees, and along the shore. Watching them, I feel suddenly protective, wondering where they have come from, wondering where they are going—wishing them Godspeed on their way.

I tiptoe carefully over the muddy path home and notice some scarlet birds clutching an evergreen tree. Their feathers blowing in the breeze, they look somehow thoughtful, with soft, glittering gazes under the great blue bowl of sky. It is as if they know it is Easter.

Spring Is Knocking
Virginia Blanck Moore

It has been pleasant, hearth,
to sit beside your fire,
but even of gold leaping flames
the heart can tire.

It has been pleasant, house,
as pleasant as can be,
your shelter from the cold
    and snow,
but walls are pressing me.

When winter comes around again,
you'll find me here once more,
but please excuse my
    absence now—
spring's knocking at my door!

Waiting
Lucille Crumley

I'm waiting for
the yellow daffodils
on tall green stalks,
and red and purple tulips
along the sunlit walks.

I'm waiting for
the warming rains
from an April sky,
the whirring of birds' wings
as they fly.

I'm waiting for
the pastel flowers
that grace the orchard trees
and the fragrant honeysuckle
that calls the golden bees.

Every Year

Eileen Spinelli

Slender branches greening,
birds in their tender-tangled nests,
creeks blessed, cool and rippling,
breezes purring,
flowers stirring into bloom.
Lovely all
falling into place
a pattern
of grace
of what could be.
Every year I see
the new
the brave
the possible.
Every year I lose my heart
to spring.

This Sudden Joy

Kay Hoffman

My heart's so full of joy today,
I want to sing and dance and play.
I do not know the reason why.
Perhaps it is the bright blue sky.
Or could it be my heart took wing
because a robin came to sing,
or that a child smiled up at me,
his face so full of impish glee?
This sudden joy my heart won't tell,
but, oh, I'm held within its spell.
Perchance the secret of this cheer
is springtime whispering in my ear.

Spring Interference
Author Unknown

No breakfast dishes
    have been washed;
I haven't made a bed.
I'm strolling down my
    garden paths,
admiring blooms instead.

There's dust upon the
    furniture,
I'm sure the floors aren't clean;
enthralled, I pick another bud,
the rarest one I've seen.

If I were prompt in
    household work,
my moments would be few
in which to see the
    morning blooms,
all shimmery with dew.

I've always tried to figure out
why pressing household duties
appear at hours when
    gardens hold
their most entrancing beauties!

Rendezvous
Mary Scott Fitzgerald

For just a brief while every day
I steal away from duty
and leave the indoor
    tasks undone,
to drench my soul in beauty.

The birdsong and the lily bells,
music thin and sweet;
sun gold and starry blooms
lavished at my feet;

cool mist, with crystal beads
gleaming everywhere;
wild plum and pink thorn
hanging on the air.

Swiftly, then, I can return
to tread the rounds of duty,
since for one fleet half
    breath I stood
hand in hand with beauty.

Sweet April showers
do spring May flowers.
—Thomas Tusser

Time for April Showers

Minnie Klemme

The skies are flying banners
and the frogfolk sing of rain.
It's time for April showers
to wash the earth again.
Soon dandelion freckles
will burst from winter's grime,
and little pansy faces
will greet the summertime.

April Puddle

Rowena Bennett

The rain falls down upon the grass
and makes a silver looking glass,
so all the buds may bend and see
what kind of flowers they will be.

PUDDLE JUMPERS *by John Sloane.*
Image © John Sloane. For information or to
order prints, visit www.johnsloaneart.com.

Life Springs Anew

Colleen Reske

I see purple buds! Within a day or two, gentle little flowers emerge, oblivious to the fact that several inches of snow are forecasted to fall within hours.

Springtime in the upper Midwest is a very welcome guest. Its arrival is long awaited and much anticipated. We spend the long winter months navigating snow-covered frozen ground, wary of nearly invisible "black ice" and the potential to lose control of our legs or vehicles at any given time. As winter progresses, the pristine white snow turns dingy along roadways, and mountains of the dirty stuff are thrust up in parking lots, eliminating parking spaces. At times, the longing to see green again becomes almost overwhelming.

We would lose all hope, except for the truth we know to be real: under the frozen blanket of winter snow, the earth is only asleep. Soon, the snow will begin to melt and the rivers and creeks will flow again. The geese, and then the cranes, will come back to the marsh as it thaws. Slowly, signs of life return as the natural world awakens in the light of an ever-warming sun.

So we wait, resting in the knowledge that springtime always follows the winter.

And just as the earth is coming back to life, we celebrate the Resurrection of our risen Christ. The parallels of springtime and Easter are striking. We grieve when the earth seems to die in the months of freezing temperatures and bone-chilling winds, yet take comfort in knowing its green rebirth is imminent. Similarly, we mourn our Savior's brutal death, then rejoice three days later at the wonder and promise of the empty tomb and Jesus' Resurrection. It is the promise that life will return that we celebrate throughout the Easter season.

This faith in new life means we are Easter people. We can live the Resurrection story at any time in our lives. We may suffer little deaths—in our relationships, our grief, and our personal journeys carrying our own crosses. But there is always hope for resurrection, which comes from knowing our Savior, Jesus Christ. He is "the way, the truth, and the life" (John 14:6, NIV).

I praise God for Jesus, giver of life everlasting. I praise God for the promise of abundant life, if only we live our lives for Him. And I praise God for springtime, and the reminder that all things can be made new in Him.

Therefore, if anyone is in Christ, he is a new creation;
the old has gone, the new has come!
—2 CORINTHIANS 5:17 NIV

An Easter Carol

Christina Rossetti

Spring bursts today,
for Christ is risen and all the earth's at play.
Flash forth, thou Sun,
the rain is over and gone, its work is done.
Winter is past,
sweet spring is come at last, is come at last.
Bud, fig and vine.
Bud, olive, fat with fruit and oil and wine.
Break forth this morn
in roses, thou but yesterday a thorn.

Uplift thy head,
O pure white lily through the winter dead.
Beside your dams
leap and rejoice, you merry-making lambs.
All herds and flocks
rejoice, all beasts of thickets and of rocks.
Sing, creatures, sing,
angels and men and birds and everything.
All notes of doves
fill all our world: this is the time of loves.

Easter Song

Mary A. Lathbury

Snowdrops! Lift your timid heads,
all the earth is waking.
Field and forest, brown and dead,
into life are waking;
snowdrops, rise, and tell the story,
how He rose, the Lord of glory.

Lilies! Lilies! Easter calls!
Rise to meet the dawning
of the blessed light that falls

through the Easter morning;
ring your bells and tell the story,
how He rose, the Lord of glory.

Waken, sleeping butterflies,
burst your narrow prison!
Spread your golden wings and rise,
for the Lord is risen;
spread your wings and tell the story,
how He rose, the Lord of glory.

Springtime Musings

J. Harold Gwynne

Buds are swelling,
    bees are telling
another spring is here;
birds are singing,
    flowers upspringing—
the gladdest time of year!

Brooks are flowing,
    breezes blowing.
The sky is azure blue;
grass is greening,
    birds are preening
as birds are wont to do.

Showers are falling,
    bluebells calling
in yonder sylvan glade;

streams are rushing,
    violets blushing
in sunkissed, dappled shade.

Lambs are skipping,
    swallows dipping
in swift and graceful flight;
leaves are quaking,
    blossoms waking.
Oh, what a pretty sight!

Hearts are praising,
    voices raising
with nature's fair rebirth;
grateful living,
    true thanksgiving
for beauties of God's earth!

Easter Carol

Author Unknown

Spring has now unwrapped
    the flow'rs;
day is fast reviving.
Life in all its fertile pow'rs
toward the light is striving.
Herb and plant that winter-long
slumbered at their leisure,
now bestirring green and strong
find in growth their pleasure!

All the world has come alive.
All the earth is budding.
Bees are humming round
    the hive,
done with winter's brooding.

Snow and frost have been
    undone.
Winds are soft and tender.
High above, the regal sun
shines in all its splendor!

This, our joy, and this, our feast,
this, our great surprising:
young and old and best and least
see their own arising.
We, the newborn patterns, are
of our God and Maker:
Christ, our spring beyond
    compare!
Christ, our good Creator!

WILD SWEET PEA AND RUFOUS HUMMINGBIRD *by Susan Bourdet. Artwork courtesy of the artist and Wild Wings (800-445-4833, www.wildwings.com).*

April Showers

Anne E. Penrod

It's beautiful in April
when the blossoms on the trees
shower sweetly-scented snowflakes
that descend upon the breeze.

From sunrise until sunset
and from darkness until dawn,
they sprinkle their enchantment
on my garden and my lawn.

It looks as if it's snowing
joy and loveliness outside,
and the countryside is glowing
like a blushing brand-new bride.

Petaled Clouds

Joy Belle Burgess

Oh, the dreams I used to weave
amidst the apple boughs,
when all the sky was white with blooms,
aglow with petaled clouds!

And each butterfly with graceful wings
seemed like a fairy queen,
who brushed against my freckled nose
while I remained unseen.

And there amongst the bees and blooms,
perched on my leafy throne,

I breathed the sweetness in the air
and heard the bees' drowsy drone;

the blithesome song a robin trilled;
the whir of a hummingbird;
but the breeze that stirred a blossom free
was the softest murmur that I heard.

And still, within my memory,
I cling amidst the boughs,
when the bursting buds of springtime
fill the sky again with petaled clouds!

I thank You, God,
for all the wealth of spring;
for gentle winds
that crooning, hurry by.
I thank You for the birds,
the songs they sing,
and for their beauty etched into the sky.
—Enola Chamberlin

New Life

Denise J. Hughes

"On the first day of the week, very early in the morning, [two women] came to the tomb, bringing the spices they had prepared. They found the stone rolled away from the tomb. They went in but did not find the body of the Lord Jesus. While they were perplexed about this, suddenly two men stood by them in dazzling clothes. So the women were terrified and bowed down to the ground. 'Why are you looking for the living among the dead?' asked the men. 'He is not here, but He has been resurrected!'"
—LUKE 24:1–6, HCSB

When I was a little girl, Easter Sunday meant a new dress. Soft pink or pale yellow, with a straw hat to match.

I knew Easter meant more than a new outfit. I knew it was the day we'd celebrate the empty tomb, and the day we'd sing "He Is Risen" in church. But I still looked forward to the new dress. Other than school clothes in September, Easter was the one time each year I got to wear something new. So on Easter Sunday, I cherished every ruffle of lace. I'd tie the ribbon (there was always a ribbon) at the back with care, making sure the bow had the perfect amount of poof. And the hat—oh, the hat! I wore it at a jaunty tilt, thinking that was how it was done.

On that first Easter when the women walked to Jesus' tomb only to find it empty, I doubt they were thinking about their clothes. The darkness that covered the earth on Friday still covered their hearts. Their hopes had been crucified with Jesus.

But then two men stood before them in dazzling clothes—angels with the most important message any ear would ever hear: "He is not here, but He has been resurrected!"

In that moment, something stirred in their spirit. New hope. New life. Jesus is alive! And they ran with all their strength back to their friends to share the amazing news.

Now we get to do the same. Not just on Easter Sunday, but every day we can share the hope we have in Christ. Jesus came to exchange our sin for His grace. His death and Resurrection give us new life.

In Ephesians 4:22–24, we're told that our old way of life has been removed, like an old garment, and we can put on our new life in Christ, like a new robe. In Revelation 19:8, we see the bride of Christ—the Church—being clothed in bright linen. It's no surprise that new clothes are a time-honored Easter tradition.

Today, I carry on the tradition with my daughters. And while I know that a new Easter dress isn't the real point, we celebrate what it represents: that because He is risen, we are robed in new life.

Hunting Easter Eggs

Vera Laurel Hoffman

The trees are showing little buds
that dance upon a bough
where rabbits' helpers hid bright eggs
and children hunt them now.

There's laughter in an open field
and eyes that fairly shine,
as children hunt the colored eggs
now that it's Eastertime.

A warm and happy time is spring,
when the early robins sing,
when children hunt for hidden eggs—
good things that Easter brings.

Easter Egg Hunt

Eleanor Lyons Culver

All over the house they scamper and run,
Tommy and Billy and Sue;
oh, they're intent on their journey of fun
searching the rooms through and through.

What do they look for, and what do they seek?
Why are they down on all fours?
Tell me why Billy and then brother Tom
glance behind all of the doors!

Now there goes Susie on short, dimpled legs
climbing a dining-room chair,
peeking where Mother's good china is kept
what does she hope to find there?

Childish laughter is filling the place,
clear to the rafters it rings.
Tommy and Billy and small sister Sue
fly just as if they have wings!

What are they finding behind Daddy's desk?
Who has the most, may I ask?
Tell me why Billy and his brother Tom
puff from their arduous task.

Now here comes Susie, my questions are done,
racing on swift sturdy legs,
swinging her basket just filled to the brim
with colorful Easter eggs.

Photograph © Nancy Matthews Photography

Rainbow Hands

Sue Davis Potts

When my daughter was little, we always dyed eggs together before Easter. She absolutely loved dipping the white eggs into the colorful cups of dye and pulling out a masterpiece a few minutes later. But one year, it was late the evening before Easter when we realized we had not dyed eggs. After a few attempts to persuade her that it would be just as fun if we did it another time, I relented, allowing her to stay up past her bedtime to dye eggs.

With the eggs boiled and cooled, garbage bags spread on the dining room table, and the flimsy little wire egg holder and colorful cups lined up, we were ready. With a look of excited determination, she began, carefully lowering the first egg into a cup of dye. Just a few excruciating seconds later, she lifted it up to see if it was dark enough yet. Of course, it wasn't. She liked the bright, vibrant colors best, and they took time to develop. This was a test of her patience. After a few more premature peeks, she slowly pulled the egg up out of the color bath, revealing a vivid purple color and prompting a look of delight on her face. Her body tensed up as she transferred her fragile piece of art with the wire holder from the cup to its holder. Her eyes met mine, and I knew that was my cue to help shield it from

falling in transit. That egg complete, my little artist was ready for the next egg, and the next, trying to make each one more beautiful than the one before.

As we sat dyeing the eggs at the dining room table, I took the opportunity to teach her about the real meaning of Easter. We talked about how eggs represent new life and that God loved us so much that He sent Jesus to give us new life. We talked about how God made the world with an astonishing array of colors. We added cross stickers to some of the eggs. I told her that even though Jesus died on the cross, the good news was He rose from the dead, and we celebrate Easter because Jesus is alive.

After we finished with the eggs, we cleaned up the table and washed our hands. Somehow my daughter only had a few splatters of dye here and there, but my own hands were covered in vivid blues and greens and reds. We scrubbed together at the bathroom sink and she got ready for bed. As I tucked her in, I looked at my hands. Some of the colors had faded, but I was still a mess. I went to bed hoping that it would wear off in the night.

But Easter morning, the vivid colors persisted. Despite my efforts and much to my embarrassment, I would be going to church

Photograph © Yuganov Konstantin/ Shutterstock.com

with rainbow hands. As I helped my daughter get into her pristine, light blue dress, she looked down and saw my hands. She squealed with excitement, grinning up at me. I smiled in return. It was then that I realized I was looking at this the wrong way. Instead of worrying about what others would think, I could see my rainbow hands as a kind of symbol, like the rainbow God gave to Noah. In them I saw a reminder of the vivid life we can live because Jesus died for us and rose that first Easter. It was also a sign that I had kept a simple promise to my little girl, by dyeing Easter eggs with her.

And so, that Easter morning, hand in colorful hand, my daughter and I walked into church. As we sang "He Lives" together, I found it impossible to be upset about the mess the dye had made. The temporary colors on my hands represented vivid, lasting memories of a special Easter together.

Remembering Easter

Andrew L. Luna

For as long as I can remember, Easter was more than just a day. It was a season of sweet traditions and anticipation, memories of which still warm my heart today.

Like many children of the sixties, my memories of Easter start a few weeks beforehand with a trip to Sears and Roebuck, where my family would purchase new outfits for Easter Sunday. My dad usually helped me find a nice suit, a new shirt, and a clip-on tie to complete the ensemble. When I emerged from the fitting room for my parents' inspection, Mom would pick at the material while pulling and yanking the sleeves, legs, and lapel in a most embarrassing way. Looking at another mother a few feet away doing the same thing to her son, I realized it must be a "mom thing."

Then, on the Saturday before Easter, my dad would hide Easter eggs around our yard for my sister and me to find. My sister was older and highly competitive, so she usually found most of the

eggs, but Dad always stood close by, encouraging me to look beside a rock or under a bush. He had two older sisters, so he understood my predicament. Finding the eggs was exciting, but eating them was less so. When I was very young, the hidden eggs were usually real. It was a bit disappointing to crack open a fancy colored egg only to discover it tasted normal.

On Easter Sunday, we all woke up to a big breakfast. Mom cooked eggs while Dad fried large slices of ham and prepared the leg of lamb for dinner, which would cook slowly in the oven while we were at church. Meanwhile, my sister and I raced to the living room where our Easter baskets waited. We were eager to dig into our candy bounty, but Mom warned us not to spoil our breakfast. We set the baskets aside, but I had to keep my Easter tradition of biting the ears off my chocolate bunny and sneaking a few malted milk balls.

After breakfast, we got dressed for church. Mom carefully inspected each of us and I often wondered if a military inspection was any worse. It was another "mom thing," though, so I just stood tall. One year, Dad gave me one of his tie bars to hold my clip-on tie securely to my shirt. I felt so grown up as Mom nodded her approval. To this day, that tie bar still sits in my jewelry box.

When we arrived at church I immediately looked for Mr. Pete, an older congregant who stood outside the sanctuary each Sunday giving pieces of candy to all the children. I loved that hard candy. Its translucent color reminded me of the pretty stained glass windows that surrounded our church. And, of course, it tasted delicious!

We started each Easter service by singing "Christ the Lord Is Risen Today," and the organ seemed to sound its happiest during this special day. The preacher spoke about newness and rebirth. There were expressions of joy and contentment on the faces of the adults, while the children daydreamed about the Easter candy awaiting them at home.

When we returned home, the smells of roast lamb, boiled potatoes, and fresh rolls had permeated our kitchen. We gathered around the table that Mom had decorated with fresh flowers and watched hungrily as Dad carved hot, juicy wedges of lamb for all of us to enjoy. When the feast was over, we ended our Easter Day in the den watching *The Robe*, *The Greatest Story Ever Told*, or *Easter Parade*, and polishing off the last of our Easter goodies.

Those Easter celebrations are decades away now. But whenever I see a decorated Easter egg, bite into a malted milk ball, or rediscover my dad's brass tie bar, I'm taken back to simpler times with my family. And I'm filled with gratitude for the joyful memories I get to claim—even all those times Mom adjusted my lapels.

A Madrigal
Clinton Scollard

Easter-glow and Easter-gleam!
Lyric laughter from the stream
that between its banks so long
murmured such a
    cheerless song;
stirrings faint and fine and thin
every woodsy place within;
root and tendril,
    bough and bole,
rousing with a throb of soul;
the old ecstasy awake
in the briar and the brake;
bluebird raptures—
    dip and run—
and the robin-antiphon;
tingling air and
    trembling earth,
and the crystal cup of mirth
brimmed and lifted to the lip
for each one of us to sip.

Dream!—'tis something
    more than dream,
Easter-glow and Easter-gleam!
Prescience 'tis and prophecy
of the wonder that shall be
when the spirit leaps to light
after death's hiemal night!

Miracles
Mary Lavinia Silvia

Cheerful little sparrow
singing in the sun,
telling the sweet story
of new springtime begun;
handsome robin redbreast
singing in a tree,
bidding us take courage,
he cheers for you and me.

Earth's reawakening
after winter's night,
spring flowers all are blooming,
a strange and sweet delight.
How could we ever view
these miracles newborn
and not believe the story
of the Resurrection morn?

New Every Morning

Anne Kennedy Brady

Every year, my in-laws host the family for Easter brunch. I look forward to sharing delicious food and sipping coffee in the spring sunshine, but for the kids, it's all about the several Easter egg hunts that take place over the course of the morning.

At my first Easter with the Bradys, the multiple hunts surprised me. When I was young, my brothers and I searched for eggs and treats only once on Easter morning, and I expected my nephews to engage in the same tradition. But upon finding all the plastic eggs scattered around the living room (Seattle rain had dampened the outdoor festivities), they cracked them open, emptied the contents into their baskets, and excitedly handed the eggs back to their grandparents.

What I initially thought was a particularly impressive display of tidying up was actually a request for round two. My in-laws set to work hiding the eggs once again while the boys dutifully covered their eyes. Once the eggs were ready, the two brothers raced to rediscover them. This routine repeated at least three times, and each time, their joy upon finding the now long-empty eggs was undimmed. I realized it was not so much the candy prizes that intrigued my young nephews. It was the thrill of discovery.

What I thought was a uniquely Brady trait turns out to be fairly universal, as I learned when we spent one Easter with my brother, his wife, and their two-year-old son, Henry. My sister-in-law had carefully selected age-appropriate gifts to hide inside each plastic egg, but, only mildly interested in their contents, Henry gleefully handed the found eggs back to his mother to hide once more. Each re-found egg elicited wide grins and hearty giggles.

As I watch the now-familiar tradition unfold each year, I'm reminded of the poet's words in Lamentations: "The steadfast love of the Lord never ceases; his mercies never come to an end; they are new every morning; great is your faithfulness." (Lamentations 3:22–23, ESV) God's love and mercy are not, in essence, new to many of us. We have heard the stories. We know the truth. And yet, when we feel His love in times of loneliness or experience His mercy in times of trouble, we cannot help but feel something akin to a young child's joy over rediscovering a treasure on Easter morning. It's something familiar. It was just in a place we didn't expect to find it.

I think about the empty tomb that Mary Magdalene and the other women discovered that first Easter morning. They had seen Jesus perform miracles throughout His ministry. They had experienced His healing firsthand. They had even seen Him raise others from the dead! And yet, upon finding His tomb empty and hearing the angels proclaim the Good News, their surprise and delight were uncontainable. I imagine their voices tumbled over each other and tears of joy spilled forth amid uncontrollable laughter. Not even the disciples' doubt could dampen their spirits, for that morning, God's mercy and love were brand-new.

This year we're celebrating Easter apart from our extended family, and we're looking forward to creating some of our own traditions. We'll attend the Easter service at our church, try to coerce our nine-month-old into something with a bow tie, invite a few friends over, and whip up a new incarnation of an old brunch favorite. And together we'll celebrate the things our young son finds new each morning—a streak of sunlight across his crib, a birdcall outside his window, a squirrel that has ventured onto our deck. And, someday, an empty plastic Easter egg, re-hidden beneath the sofa.

Easy Easter Monkey Bread

1   cup granulated sugar
2   tablespoons ground
      cinnamon, divided
3   tubes of large refrigerated
      biscuits (10 to a package)

Raisins and/or nuts (optional)
½   cup butter, melted
1   cup brown sugar

Preheat oven to 350°F. Place sugar and 1 tablespoon cinnamon in a zippered plastic bag and shake to mix. Cut each biscuit into thirds and toss biscuit pieces in bag with sugar-cinnamon mixture until all pieces are coated. Place sugar-coated biscuit pieces in well-greased Bundt pan or angel food cake pan. Add raisins and/or nuts among the biscuits if desired. In small bowl, mix melted butter, brown sugar, and remaining cinnamon together and pour over biscuits in pan. Bake for 35 minutes. Let stand 10 minutes before serving. Invert pan on a serving plate and lift off to serve. Makes 10 to 12 servings.

Family Recipes

Kolaches

1 cup sour cream
½ cup granulated sugar
1½ teaspoons salt
½ cup unsalted butter
1 packet active dry yeast
½ cup warm water (110° to 115°F)
3 eggs, divided
4 to 4½ cups all-purpose flour
Apricot Filling (recipe follows)

In a small pan over medium-low heat, combine the first 4 ingredients, stirring, until butter melts. Cool to 110° to 115°F. In a separate bowl, sprinkle yeast over warm water; let stand 5 minutes. In a large bowl, stir together yeast mixture, sour cream mixture, and 2 eggs. Add flour, a cup at a time, until a soft dough is formed. On a lightly floured surface, knead until smooth and elastic, about 6 to 8 minutes. Place in a greased bowl. Cover and let rise in a warm place until doubled, about 1 hour.

Punch dough down. Divide in half; divide each half into 12 pieces and shape into balls. Place 3 inches apart on baking sheets lined with parchment paper. Flatten each ball to a 3-inch circle. Make a depression in the center of each roll. Cover and let rise in a warm place, about 30 minutes.

Preheat oven to 350°F. Spoon 1 tablespoon filling into depression of each roll. Combine egg and 1 tablespoon water; brush edges of pastry with egg wash. Bake 14 to 17 minutes or until golden brown. Remove from pan to cool on a wire rack. Makes 2 dozen.

APRICOT FILLING

1 cup dried apricots, snipped into ¼-inch pieces
½ cup granulated sugar
½ teaspoon finely grated lemon zest
¼ teaspoon ground cinnamon
1 teaspoon cornstarch
1 tablespoon lemon juice
1 tablespoon butter

In a small saucepan, add apricots and just enough water to cover and let sit for one hour. Mix in sugar, cinnamon, and lemon zest. Bring to a boil. Reduce heat and simmer for 15 minutes. Stir cornstarch into lemon juice and add to pan. Simmer 15 minutes or until filling thickens. Remove from heat and stir in butter. Cool to lukewarm before using.

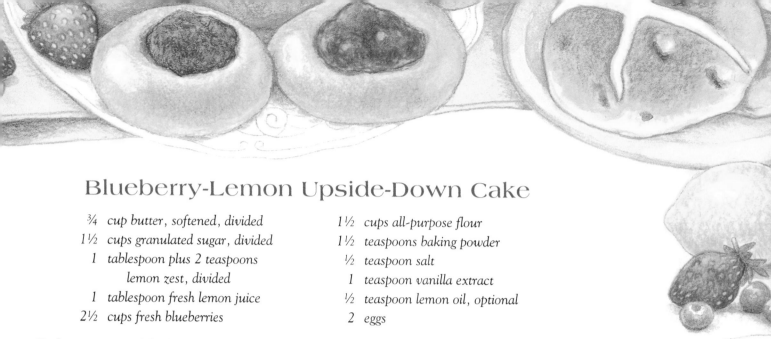

Blueberry-Lemon Upside-Down Cake

¾ cup butter, softened, divided
1½ cups granulated sugar, divided
1 tablespoon plus 2 teaspoons
    lemon zest, divided
1 tablespoon fresh lemon juice
2½ cups fresh blueberries

1½ cups all-purpose flour
1½ teaspoons baking powder
½ teaspoon salt
1 teaspoon vanilla extract
½ teaspoon lemon oil, optional
2 eggs

Preheat oven to 350°F. In a small pan over medium heat, melt ¼ cup butter. Add ½ cup sugar, 2 teaspoons lemon zest, and lemon juice. Bring mixture to boil; reduce heat and simmer for 2 minutes. Pour into a buttered 9-inch cake pan. Spread blueberries over base of pan, pressing them down with the palm of your hand. In a medium bowl, sift together flour, baking powder, and salt; set aside. In a large bowl, cream remaining butter and sugar until light and fluffy. Add remaining lemon zest, vanilla, and lemon oil, and beat until well mixed. Beat in eggs, one at a time. Add flour mixture slowly, mixing until blended. Spoon batter evenly over blueberries. Bake 45 to 50 minutes, until cake is firm to the touch. Cool in pan 10 minutes; invert onto serving plate. Makes 8 to 10 servings.

Easy Easter Brunch Casserole

1 pound bulk breakfast sausage
1 large onion, chopped
1 cup diced green and red bell peppers
6 slices bread, cubed

6 eggs
1½ cups milk
   Salt and black pepper
1 cup shredded Cheddar cheese

In a large skillet over medium-high heat, brown sausage, stirring occasionally. Add onions and peppers, and cook until softened. Drain grease and set aside. Place bread cubes into a greased 11 x 7 x 2-inch baking dish. Sprinkle sausage mixture over bread. In a medium bowl, whisk together eggs and milk. Add salt and pepper to taste. Pour over sausage, pressing mixture down until bread is moist. Sprinkle cheese on top. Cover and refrigerate overnight.

Preheat oven to 375°F. Bake, uncovered, 40 to 45 minutes or until brown and puffy. Cool 10 minutes; cut into squares to serve. Makes 6 to 8 servings.

Stuck on Saturday

Dena Johnson

It's Saturday. The day between the Crucifixion and the Resurrection.

I woke with the disciples on my mind, wondering what they must have been thinking, feeling, and experiencing. They had watched their friend, their teacher, their Savior hang on a cross and breathe His last breath.

Dying with that breath must have been their dreams, their hopes, their expectations. Everything they had believed was now gone, and they had all scattered. How quickly their faith died with Jesus.

And Peter. Bold, outspoken Peter. Zealous Peter, who had cut off the ear of the high priest's slave. Peter, who vowed never to leave Jesus, but to stay with Him to the end. The same Peter who a short time later denied even knowing Him. Where was he on Saturday? Was he hiding in shame and humiliation? Was he alone, sulking? Was he wondering how he could have been so gullible as to believe Jesus? Was he simply trying to make sense of everything that had happened?

When I walked outside early this morning, it was cloudy—dark and overcast. The silence was deafening, and I could imagine how the disciples must have felt on Saturday. They had walked the streets of Jerusalem with Jesus for three years, sacrificing everything to follow Him. And now He was gone. No more peaceful dinners listening to Jesus share truths they longed to hear. No more stories with deeper hidden meanings. No more fellowship. Only heavy darkness and ear-piercing silence.

They didn't know Sunday was coming.

You see, we have the benefit of knowing the rest of the story—the glorious Resurrection. We know that Christ didn't stay in that tomb. We know that He is risen!

But how many of us today are stuck on Saturday, just like the disciples? We live our lives in a gloom when promises get broken or expectations are unmet. We wonder where our Savior has gone. We scatter at the slightest hint of disappointment, because we feel deserted.

I've been there. I know what it is to feel like God is silent. And yet, as believers, we have hope that Sunday is coming. We have the benefit of knowing the rest of the story. We know that God keeps His promises, because we've seen how He fulfilled every word He ever spoke. In times of trouble, we must remember that our faith is built on the Resurrection—the truth that not even the chains of death can stop God. He can restore every loss and every pain.

So cling to the promise that He's not finished. There is more to our story, and as long as we have breath in our lungs, God is writing it. You may not see Him working. You may not hear Him. But He is there, arranging circumstances to fulfill His promises and His purposes, in your life and in mine.

One day soon, the earth will shake. The mountains will tremble. The stone will roll away. The darkness will give way to glorious light that can only come from our Savior. We will see the rest of the story unfold.

Prayer in Gethsemane

Matthew 26:36–46

THEN cometh Jesus with them unto a place called Gethsemane, and saith unto the disciples, Sit ye here, while I go and pray yonder. And he took with him Peter and the two sons of Zebedee, and began to be sorrowful and very heavy.

Then saith he unto them, My soul is exceeding sorrowful, even unto death: tarry ye here, and watch with me. And he went a little farther, and fell on his face, and prayed, saying, O my Father, if it be possible, let this cup pass from me: nevertheless not as I will, but as thou wilt.

And he cometh unto the disciples, and findeth them asleep, and saith unto Peter, What, could ye not watch with me one hour? Watch and pray, that ye enter not into temptation: the spirit indeed is willing, but the flesh is weak.

He went away again the second time, and prayed, saying, O my Father, if this cup may not pass away from me, except I drink it, thy will be done.

And he came and found them asleep again: for their eyes were heavy. And he left them, and went away again, and prayed the third time, saying the same words.

Then cometh he to his disciples, and saith unto them, Sleep on now, and take your rest: behold, the hour is at hand, and the Son of man is betrayed into the hands of sinners. Rise, let us be going: behold, he is at hand that doth betray me.

Crucified at Golgotha

Mark 15:20–28

AND when they had mocked him, they took off the purple from him, and put his own clothes on him, and led him out to crucify him.

And they compel one Simon a Cyrenian, who passed by, coming out of the country, the father of Alexander and Rufus, to bear his cross.

And they bring him unto the place Golgotha, which is, being interpreted, The place of a skull. And they gave him to drink wine mingled with myrrh: but he received it not.

And when they had crucified him, they parted his garments, casting lots upon them, what every man should take.

And it was the third hour, and they crucified him.

And the superscription of his accusation was written over, THE KING OF THE JEWS.

And with him they crucify two thieves; the one on his right hand, and the other on his left.

And the scripture was fulfilled, which saith, And he was numbered with the transgressors.

Stained glass by F. Zettler at the German Church in Stockholm, Sweden.
Photograph © jorisvo/Shutterstock.com

He Is Risen

Mark 16:1–6

AND when the sabbath was past, Mary Magdalene, and Mary the mother of James, and Salome, had bought sweet spices, that they might come and anoint him.

And very early in the morning the first day of the week, they came unto the sepulchre at the rising of the sun.

And they said among themselves, Who shall roll us away the stone from the door of the sepulchre? And when they looked, they saw that the stone was rolled away: for it was very great.

And entering into the sepulchre, they saw a young man sitting on the right side, clothed in a long white garment; and they were affrighted.

And he saith unto them, Be not affrighted: Ye seek Jesus of Nazareth, which was crucified: he is risen; he is not here: behold the place where they laid him.

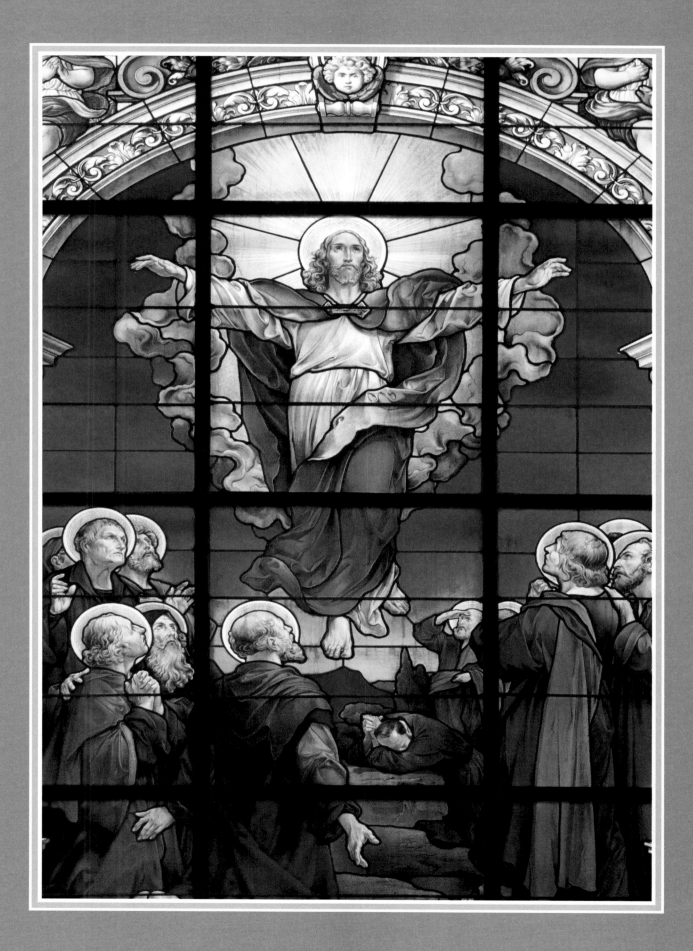

Through My Window

Joanna's Story

Pamela Kennedy

I received your letter, Luke, requesting that I share with you my experiences as a follower of Jesus. As I grow older, it seems good that there should be some record of what He meant to me. Thus, although it may not be eloquent, I pray this recollection is helpful as you compose your account of the life of our Lord.

At the age of fifteen I was married to Chuza, the manager of the household of Herod Antipas, the king of Galilee. By all accounts it was a good match, for my husband was rich and I lived in the splendor of the court at Tiberias. But, plagued by illness, I did not please my husband. And therein lay the source of both my greatest pain and my greatest joy.

Let me explain. It was in the court that I first heard of Jesus. His cousin, John the Baptizer, had been dragged in chains before Herod to testify. The king was jealous of John's fame and insulted by his accusations, but also intrigued by his fervent teaching. When John was called to respond to Herod's questions, those of us living in the household heard him speak about Jesus of Nazareth—that He had power to heal the sick and even raise the dead! As I listened, I felt the blossoming of a hope I had never thought to know.

When word spread that Jesus would be visiting Capernaum, I gathered some friends and traveled there. Arriving at sunset, we found Him outside the home of a fisherman named Peter. People brought their sick and dying to Jesus, and He prayed over them, laying His hands on them. I don't know what compelled me, but I couldn't keep still. I crept forward through the crowd. Then, without warning, a gentle hand rested on my head. Warmth, unlike I had ever experienced, coursed through my body and I gasped, glancing up. Deep brown eyes gazed into mine and I heard a voice say, "My daughter, be healed." Fear, pain, and anxiety fled, and a peaceful joy I had never known flooded my heart. I knew this man was everything John had claimed.

Returning to the court, I told everyone of my transformation. But in my brief absence, things had changed. John had been murdered, and speaking of him or of Jesus was now forbidden. Chuza feared that my newfound belief in Jesus as Messiah would cause Herod to banish us from court. Thus, in order to protect his livelihood and position, he decided to divorce me, but to honor my right of Ketubah—a sum of money promised to a Jewish wife in case of divorce. So what should have brought me shame became my salvation! Now, liberated and with funds of my own, I was free to follow Jesus.

I joined with Mary of Magdala, Susanna, and other women healed by Jesus who felt called to support His ministry. Together we traveled with

the twelve, purchasing and preparing their food, securing lodging, serving in whatever way the Master needed. It was an experience of both love and learning. In His presence and among His followers the strict regulations of society fell away. There was neither slave nor free, man nor woman, poor nor rich. We were all loved. The Teacher reminded us that whatever we did for anyone, however lowly, we did for Him.

When the time of His ultimate sacrifice arrived as He had promised, we grieved, but not without hope. He had told us He would return, and because of who He was, we believed. So we watched, on that bleak Golgotha hillside, as soldiers nailed Him on a cross between two thieves. We experienced the darkness and the earthquake and heard Him call out, "It is finished!" But I knew it wasn't. Nothing was ever what it seemed with my Savior. We followed as Joseph of Arimathea wrapped the body in linen and carried it to his own tomb. We noted where it was, determined to return on the first day of the week.

That morning, before sunrise, we gathered the spices and oils we had prepared and walked to the garden tomb. But we did not find the body of our Lord. Instead we encountered two angels, gleaming like lightning! As we bowed to the ground they spoke: "Why do you look for the living among the dead? He is not here; He has risen! Remember how He told you, while He was still with you in Galilee: 'The Son of Man must be delivered into the hands of sinful men, be crucified, and on the third day be raised again.'"

We ran to the disciples, shouting the good news. Assuming we were hysterical from grief, they refused to believe us. But we knew. We knew that He who had given us new life could not be held by the grave.

That is what I want you to write in your account, dear Dr. Luke. This is the Lord we serve: He is the One who creates greatness from small things, who defies earthly limitations, who refutes human judgments about what is important and what is not. He brings health to the sick, hope to the hopeless, and life to the dead. Neither chains of prejudice nor tombs of stone can hold Him. He is alive—forever!

Joy So Wonderful
Keith H. Graham

Visit the stable
under starry skies;
with peace in your voices,
with peace in your eyes,
look in the manger
where Immanuel lies.

Stand on the hillside
under stormy skies;
with grief in your voices,
with grief in your eyes,
look to the cross
where the Savior dies.

Enter the garden
under sunny skies;
with joy in your voices,
with joy in your eyes,
look in the tomb
where God made His Son rise.

Oh, the Easter bells are gladly ringing;
let the whole world join the happy lay!
Let the hills and vales break forth in singing,
"Christ, the Lord of Life, is ris'n today!"
—Lizzie Akers

Easter Day
Felicia Dorothea Hemans

Christ hath arisen! O mountain peaks, attest—
witness, resounding glen and torrent wave!
The immortal courage in the human breast
sprung from that victory—tell how oft the brave
to camp midst rock and cave,
nerved by those words, their struggling faith have borne,
planting the cross on high above the clouds of morn!

Lime tree at sunrise in Bavaria, Germany. Photograph © Raimund Linke/Masterfile, Inc.

Easter Prayer
Esther Lloyd Dauber

May I experience on this day
a resurrection, Lord,
a resurrection of goodwill,
of love and sweet accord.
May all the good that dwells within
become alive in me,
that someone on this Easter Day
may catch a glimpse of Thee.

An Easter Prayer
Charles Hanson Towne

Lord, now that spring is in the world
and every tulip is a cup
filled with the wine of Thy great love,
lift Thou me up.

Raise Thou my heart as flowers rise
to greet the glory of Thy day,
with soul as clean as lilies are,
and white as they.

Let me not fear the darkness now,
since life and light break through Thy tomb;
teach me that doubts no more oppress,
no more consume.

Show me Thou art April, Lord,
and Thou the flowers and the grass;
then, when awake the soft spring winds,
I'll hear Thee pass!

Easter Triumph

Lucille Crumley

Easter is a story of discovery—the discovery that Christ lives. That fact has freed us from the deep fear of death.

How disappointed the disciples must have been that last day of Jesus' life. Calvary seemed to them an irretrievable disaster. Their last act of love was to prepare His body for burial, and not a single disciple believed He would live again.

Then, out of the gloom of the garden came glorious news: "He is risen." Suddenly the disciples were no longer alone! Jesus had walked back into their lives, and death had not changed Him. His love had not ended. His compassion had not cooled. He knew Mary by her voice, Peter by his faults, and Thomas by his doubts.

Christ was not a memory, but a presence. When doors close and life tumbles in, when hope no longer sees a star, there comes a voice saying, "Be not afraid. I live."

And because He lives, we, too, shall live again. If Christianity had ended on the cross, we should never have heard of it. Instead, Easter changes a martyrdom into a coronation. On Good Friday, the world said, "No." On Easter Sunday, God said, "Yes."

IN GREEN PASTURES *by Yongsung Kim.*
Image © Yongsung Kim/GoodSalt

A Divine Collaboration

Pamela Kennedy

Some hymns are the result of lightning bolts of inspiration, while others come from hours of meditation. But this hymn was the result of holy coincidence!

In the spring of 1865, John Thomas Grape, the organist at the Monument Street Methodist Church of Baltimore, Maryland, composed a new tune for a hymn written by William Bradbury. He titled it, "All To Thee I Owe." Satisfied with his composition, Grape gave his melody to the church's pastor, Reverend George Schrick. After some consideration, Pastor Schrick tucked the melody away in a file, unconvinced that it was the right vehicle for Bradbury's words.

Later that same spring, while listening to one of Reverend Schrick's sermons, a choir member, Elvina Hall, became inspired by her pastor's words regarding God's forgiveness and Christ's sacrifice on the cross to secure salvation for believers. Elvina felt compelled to write down her thoughts in verse. Unfortunately, sitting in the choir loft, she was without paper. What she did have, however, was a hymnal. Opening it to the blank flyleaf, Elvina hastily scribbled the four verses of a poem, each verse ending in a chorus that echoed the pastor's theme.

When the service ended, Elvina waited until the parishioners departed, then approached Reverend Schrick. Apologizing for her inattention during his sermon, as well as for defacing a church hymnal, she handed him the book, opened to her handwritten verses. As he read the words, a strange look came over the pastor's face. Dashing to his study, he quickly located the melody given to him earlier by John Grape. Amazingly, the poem written by Elvina Hall perfectly matched the notes as well as the title of Grape's tune.

Three years later, in 1868, Reverend Schrick had the hymn published in a collection entitled *Sabbath Carols*. Since that time, "Jesus Paid It All" has been included in gospel song-books and hymnals around the world.

In God's perfect timing, an amateur organist composed a melody that fit a poem not yet written by a volunteer choir member. Then they both gave their work to a pastor who brought the two together to produce a beautiful musical tribute to God's redemptive work. How perfect, then, that the chorus reminds the singer of the true Author by affirming, "All to Him I owe!"

Jesus Paid It All

Elvina M. Hall (lyrics) John T. Grape (music)

1. I hear the Sav - ior say, "Thy strength in - deed is small;
2. Lord, now in - deed I find Thy power, and Thine a - lone,
3. For noth - ing good have I where - by Thy grace to claim—
4. And when be - fore the throne I stand in Him com - plete,

Child of weak - ness, watch and pray, find in Me thine all in all."
Can change the lep - er's spots and melt the heart of stone.
I'll wash my gar - ments white in the blood of Cal - vary's Lamb.
"Je - sus died my soul to save," my lips shall still re - peat.

Je - sus paid it all, all to Him I owe;

Sin had left a crim-son stain, He washed it white as snow.

Upward
Pamela Love

Slender steeples
point the way
to heaven above
on Easter Day.

Lilies' fragrance
upward soars,

both in church
and out-of-doors.

Christians' voices
fill the air
with melody
and Easter prayer.

Sunrise Service
Pamela Love

Our eyes may look sleepy,
our clothes, not quite neat.
We may stifle a yawn.
We might shuffle our feet.

But music and gospel
together combine

to waken our hearts
at this glorious time.

And though it's still early,
with minds now awake,
we give thanks to Jesus
who died for our sake.

Country Church
Ray I. Hoppman

A small church in the
   country,
built on a sloping hill
in nature's rich surroundings,
beside a rippling rill . . .
a special time for singing,
to bow the head and pray,
for it was Easter Sunday,
the hallelujah day.

The congregation entered,
the secton rang the bell,
the parson preached
   the sermon
all of them knew so well:
the Resurrection story,
with faith renewed to hear.
It was the Easter Sunday
when God seemed very near.

Bits & Pieces

The bluebird carries
the sky on his back.
—Henry David Thoreau

The robin flew from his swinging spray of ivy onto the
top of the wall and he opened his beak and sang a loud,
lovely trill, merely to show off. Nothing in the world is
quite as adorably lovely as a robin when he shows off—
and they are nearly always doing it.
—Frances Hodgson Burnett, The Secret Garden

They'll come again to the apple tree—
robin and all the rest—
when the orchard branches are fair to see
in the snow of the blossoms dressed;
and the prettiest thing in the world will be
the building of the nest.
—Margaret E. Sangster

In almost everything
that touches our everyday
life on earth, God is pleased
when we're pleased. He wills
that we be as free as birds to
soar and sing our Maker's
praise without anxiety.
—Aiden Wilson Tozer

My favorite
weather is
bird-chirping
weather.
—Terri Guillemets

I realized that if I had to choose,
I would rather have birds than airplanes.
—Charles Lindbergh

Hear how the birds, on
every blooming spray,
with joyous music wake
the dawning day!
—Alexander Pope

The reason birds fly, and we can't, is
simply that they have perfect faith, for
to have perfect faith is to have wings.
—James M. Barrie

The nightingale appeared the first,
and as her melody she sang,
the apple into blossom burst,
to life the grass and
    violets sprang.
—Heinrich Heine

When the groundhog casts his shadow
and the small birds sing
and the pussy willows happen
and the sun shines warm
and when the peepers peep
then it is spring.
—Margaret Wise Brown

Easter Songs

Keith H. Graham

Purple blooms dot grassy seas
where playful children run,
seeking "sunken treasure" eggs
under the rising sun.

Loud laughter
is the song they sing,
Easter morning,
early spring.

Birds perch on flowered branches
in a grove of pinkish trees,
spreading cheery celebration
on wings of a gentle breeze.

Pleasant sounds
are the song they sing,
Easter morning,
early spring.

People bow heads in a country church
amidst the scents of flowers,
thankful for the Resurrection,
and blessings like spring showers.

Heartfelt praises
are the song they sing,
Easter morning,
early spring.

Angels gather at the Savior's throne,
then bowing at His feet,
sing, "Hallelujah! You are risen!"—
up and down the golden street.

His song
is the song they sing,
Resurrection morning,
early spring.

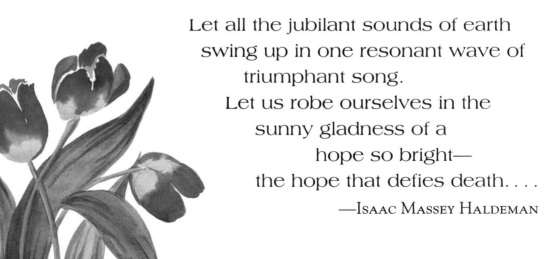

Let all the jubilant sounds of earth
swing up in one resonant wave of
triumphant song.
Let us robe ourselves in the
sunny gladness of a
hope so bright—
the hope that defies death. . . .

—Isaac Massey Haldeman

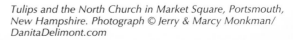

Tulips and the North Church in Market Square, Portsmouth, New Hampshire. Photograph © Jerry & Marcy Monkman/ DanitaDelimont.com

A Light Upon the Mountains

Henry Burton

There's a light upon the mountains,
and the day is at the spring,
when our eyes shall see the beauty
and the glory of the King;
weary was our heart with waiting,
and the night-watch seemed so long,
but His triumph-day is breaking,
and we hail it with a song.
In the fading of the starlight
we may see the coming morn;
and the lights of men are paling
in the splendors of the dawn;
for the eastern skies are glowing
as with light of hidden fire,
and the hearts of men are stirring
with the throbs of deep desire.

There's a hush of expectation
and a quiet in the air,
and the breath of God is moving
in the fervent breath of prayer;
for the suffering, dying Jesus
is the Christ upon the throne,
and the travail of our spirit
is the travail of His own.
Hark! We hear a distant music,
and it comes with fuller swell;
'tis the triumph-song of Jesus,
of our King Immanuel!
Go ye forth with joy to meet Him!
And, my soul, be swift to bring
all thy sweetest and thy dearest
for the triumph of our King.

This Is My Father's World

Maltbie D. Babcock

This is my Father's world,
and to my listening ears
all nature sings, and round me rings
the music of the spheres.
This is my Father's world:
I rest me in the thought
of rocks and trees, of skies and seas;
His hand the wonders wrought.
This is my Father's world;
the birds their carols raise;
the morning light, the lily white,
declare their Maker's praise.
This is my Father's world:

He shines in all that's fair.
In the rustling grass I hear Him pass;
He speaks to me everywhere.
This is my Fathers world,
Oh! Let me ne'er forget
that though the wrong
    seems oft so strong,
God is the Ruler yet.
This is my Father's world:
the battle is not done;
Jesus who died shall be satisfied,
and earth and heaven be one.

A Prayer for Joy at Easter

Rebecca Barlow Jordan

Lord, send your blessings and your best
to each one, great and small.
Let them know that Easter Day
was given for them all.
Touch with resurrection power
and fill each life again;
renew each heart with happiness
and bring new joy within.

ISBN-13: 978-0-8249-1351-9

Published by Ideals
An imprint of Worthy Publishing Group
A division of Worthy Media, Inc.
Nashville, Tennessee

Printed and bound in the U.S.A.
Printed on Weyerhaeser Lynx. The paper used in this publication meets the minimum requirements of American National Standard for Information Sciences—Permanence of Paper for Printed Materials, ANSI Z39.48-1984.

Publisher, Peggy Schaefer
Editor, Melinda L. R. Rumbaugh
Copy Editors, Anne Kennedy Brady, Olivia Forehand
Designer, Marisa Jackson
Permissions and Research, Kristi West

Cover: Photograph © Robert Mabic/Gap Photos, Inc.
Inside front cover: HOEING TEAM AND IRIS FIELDS, 1993 by Timothy Easton. Image © Timothy Easton/Private Collection/Bridgeman Images
Inside back cover: IRISES AND SUMMER HOUSE SHADOWS, 1996 by Timothy Easton. Image © Timothy Easton/Private Collection/Bridgeman Images
Sheet music for "Jesus Paid It All" by Dick Torrans, Melode, Inc. Additional art credits: Pages 1, 36–37, 54, 58–59, and back cover art by Kathryn Rusynyk.

Join the community of *Ideals* readers on Facebook at: www.facebook.com/IdealsMagazine
Readers are invited to submit original poetry and prose for possible use in future publications. Please send no more than four typed submissions to:
Ideals submissions, Worthy Publishing Group, 6100 Tower Circle, Suite 210, Franklin, Tennessee 37067. Manuscripts will be returned if a self-adressed, stamped envelope is included.

ACKNOWLEDGMENTS:

HUGHES, DENISE J. "New Life" from www.incourage.me. All rights reserved. Used by permission of the author. JOHNSON, DENA. "Stuck on Saturday" from www.crosswalk.com/blogs/denajohnson. All rights reserved. Used by permission. RESKE, COLLEEN. "Life Springs Anew" from www.hopetofind.blogspot.com. All rights reserved. Used by permission of the author. OUR THANKS to the following authors or their heirs: Deborah A. Bennett, Rowena Bennett, Anne Kennedy Brady, Joy Belle Burgess, Enola Chamberlin, Thomas Curtis Clark, Eleanor Lyons Culver, Lucille Crumley, Esther Lloyd Dauber, Keith H. Graham, J. Harold Gwynne, Kay Hoffman, Vera Laurel Hoffman, Ray I. Hoppman, Edna Jaques, Rebecca Barlow Jordan, Pamela Kennedy, Minnie Klemme, Pamela Love, Andrew L. Luna, Virginia Blanck Moore, Anne E. Penrod, Sue Davis Potts, Mary Lavinia Silvia, Eileen Spinelli, and Susan Sundwall.

Scripture quotations, unless otherwise indicated, are taken from King James Version (KJV). Scripture quotations marked NIV are taken from The Holy Bible, New International Version®, NIV® Copyright © 1973, 1978, 1984, 2011 by Biblica, Inc.® Used by permission. All rights reserved worldwide. Scripture quotation marked HCSB is taken from Holman Christian Standard Bible (HCSB) Copyright © 1999, 2000, 2002, 2003, 2009 by Holman Bible Publishers, Nashville Tennessee. All rights reserved. Scripture quotation marked ESV is taken from the Holy Bible, English Standard Version. Copyright © 2001 by Crossway, a publishing ministry of Good News Publishers. Used by permission. All rights reserved.

Every effort has been made to establish ownership and use of each selection in this book. If contacted, the publisher will be pleased to rectify any inadvertent errors or omissions in subsequent editions.